When Winners Don't Win

By Mark Elefane
Illustrated by Dante Fernandez

Text copyright © 2023 by Mark Elefane

Illustration copyright © 2023 by Dante Fernandez

Print ISBN: 979-8-9890518-0-9

All rights reserved. No part of this book may be used, reproduced, stored in a retrieval system, or transmitted in any form by any means, including mechanical, electronic, photocopy, recording, scanning, and methods not invented or in common use at the time of this publication, without the prior written consent of the publisher.

Library of Congress Control Number: 2023919928

Published in 2023 by Elefane Media, Orlando, FL

Printed in the United States of America

This book is dedicated to the many people who inspired it and helped it along the way: Robyn, Emma, Evan, The Links, Andrew, Dante, and my students who give it their all to better themselves and the world around them.

Winners will work
And winners will play
They practice and train
All night and all day

Some of them win
With a team of supporters
Some battle alone
With a team in their corner

Winners can win
On a court or a field
Some on a board,
In a ring, or on wheels

And other ways too
If you dare to begin
But one thing is true
Winners don't always win

Yes that's correct
Winners can bruise
They can miss, they can fall
Winners can lose

It doesn't feel great
When you don't finish first
The more that you care
The more that it hurts

FRUSTRATED, MAD
The feelings are strong
And they all feel bad
Don't let them last long

They'll smother and hold you
And eat up your pride
For as long as you let them
They'll twist you inside

You may want to scream
Or push people away
Or say things out loud
That you don't mean to say

Or have thoughts in your head
That pull at your heart
And make you believe
That you're falling apart

You'll question it all
In a fit of emotion
You might think of quitting
You might think you're broken

But whatever you do
It's important to wait
Til you're back in control
And your head is on straight

If you've gotten that far
You can start to relax
You're calm and you're clear
It's time to come back

You can study and see
How technique improves
And things you can do
To work on your moves

You have new perspective
And new lessons learned
With new things to practice
For wins that you'll earn

If you use that new knowledge
To take some new measures
Then losing can teach you
And help you get better

When winners don't win
It's a well known fact
There's still a right way
That a winner should act

Complaining and blaming
Do no good at all
But they make a competitor
Appear very small

Instead, be big
You can still be upset
But the players and the game
Deserve your respect

Respect for the work
That makes it all happen
Respect for each soul
That's sharing your passion

Respect for the people
Who love you no less
Who can watch you not win
And still say you're the best

And they truly believe it
Through anger or sorrow
They're all on your side
And they'll still be tomorrow

They're cheering you on
Each time that you try
No need to ask
No need to ask why

Fans, family
Teammates and friends
One hundred percent
All the way to the end

If the loss is still heavy
And you're still feeling beaten
Sometimes it helps
To think of your reason

Why do you do it
All this work to compete
Why push yourself through
Such tough goals to meet

Some do it for the challenge
Some do it for the team
Some do it for a feeling
Some say it's their dream

It could be one of those
It might be a few
And even in defeat
The reasons stay true

You can still be a champion
It's part of the cost
There's never been a champ
Who's never ever lost

The heroes, the idols
All of the greats
They've all had bad days
And learned from mistakes

They picked themselves up
And brushed off the dirt
Recovered and healed
And went back to work

Onward and upward
Keeping in view
The next tough task
It's what winners do

It's a difficult thing
To put yourself to the test
But it makes you better
You could be the best

You'll grow and you'll build
In more ways than one
And with the right attitude
It'll keep being fun

Just keep taking steps
No matter the size
A chance to advance
Is a chance to rise

And rise you will
To as high as you'll go
Meeting people and places
You'll be happy to know

It's good to remember
To learn from the past
Defeats can repeat
This may not be the last

They'll all be difficult
But worth it, believe me
If something is awesome
It's likely not easy

If you ever fall short
You're not a loser quite yet
It all just depends
On what you do next

For fun or for real
Pro or beginner
Win, lose, or tie
Go be a winner!

The End

www.ingramcontent.com/pod-product-compliance
Lightning Source LLC
LaVergne TN
LVHW072054070426
835508LV00002B/91